Things Every Kid Should Know

STRANGERS!

ZAFAR NURI

EMAN
publishing

Eman Publishing
P.O. Box 404
FISHERS, IN 46038
www.emanpublishing.com

Order Online: www.zafarnuri.com

ISBN 13: 978-0-9841275-4-2
ISBN 10: 0-9841275-4-2

Cover Design by Saqib Shaikh

Printed in the United States of America

Things Every Kid Should Know

STRANGERS!

ZAFAR NURI

Al and Bart were playing soccer in the park. They were having so much fun that they were not paying attention to what was happening around them. They didn't notice that two men were hiding behind some nearby bushes.

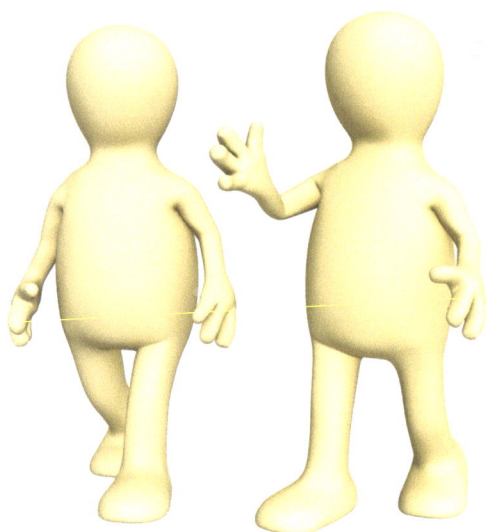

They also didn't notice that the two men were sneaking up to kidnap them.

Suddenly, the strangers grabbed at them!

Al and Bart knew something was wrong. They stopped playing soccer and turned to run away from the strangers. They ran home as fast as they could, screaming, "Call 911!" all the way.

The strangers heard the boys yelling; so they went back to their car to go home. The strangers were mad.

3

The neighbor, Mr. Johnson was standing on his balcony. He saw Al and Bart running and heard them screaming, "Call 911!" So Mr. Johnson rushed inside and called 911.

The neighbor told the police that two guys were chasing the boys; he also tried to describe what the guys looked like.

The boys ran to their homes as quickly as they could.

Suddenly, the police came and looked for the strangers; they found them in their car.

They went to their car and asked them to get out and took the strangers to jail.

When Bart had gotten home, he told his mom, "Mom, there was a strange man in the park and he tried to grab me. Another strange man tried to grab Al!"

Bart's mom asked, "What happened to Al?" Bart said, "He ran home."

His mom said, "Let's call Al's house to make sure he made it home okay." Bart's mom called Al's house, and Al was home safe too. Bart's mom said, "Next time I don't want you to go to the park without a parent." **Bart agreed.**

Then Bart's mom called the police to tell them about what happened.

Then, Mr. Johnson, Al and Bart were asked to see the strangers, to make sure that it was them who tried to kidnap them.

Bart's mom was proud of Bart, because Bart ran away from the strangers, and he yelled 'Call 911'.

WHO ARE
STRANGERS?

A stranger is someone you don't know.

1. **What should you do if a stranger comes up to you?**
    Stand up and quickly move away from him or her. If the stranger follows you, you should run as fast as you can, and scream, "Call 911".

2. **What should you do if a stranger talks to you?**
    Keep quiet. Never tell them your phone number, address, and name.

3. **What should you do if a stranger comes closer to you?**
    Move further away from the stranger. Try to go to a place where you know someone.

4. **What should you do if a stranger wants to give you something?**
    Do not take it.

5. **What should you do if a stranger asks for help?**
    Do not help him or her.

6. **What is the best thing to do when a stranger comes to talk to you?**
Run as fast as you can in the opposite direction and scream "Call 911!"

Have You Bought The Series, "Things Every Kid Should Know: Smoking, Drugs, Alcohol and Bullying" for Your Kids?

Written By A "9 Year Old" Author
Alya Nuri

www.ThingsEveryKidShouldKnow.com

www.AlyaNuri.com

Things Every Kid Should Know Drugs!

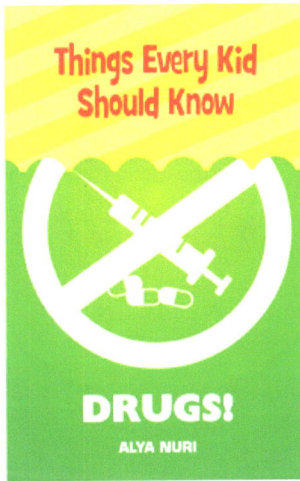

'Things Every Kid Should Know - Drugs!' will walk you through what Drugs are; why they are bad for you, and how to avoid picking up this bad habit. There is a story of a young man who goes through his high school doing drugs, and what happens in his life due to making that choice. There are also facts in the story to help understand the issue of Drugs.

Things Every Kid Should Know
Alcohol!

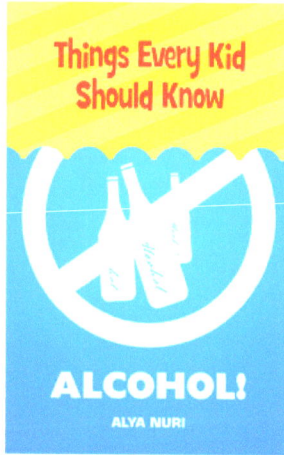

'Things Every Kid Should Know - Alcohol!' will walk you through what Alcohol is; why it is bad for you, and how to avoid picking up this bad habit. There is a story of a girl who discovers Alcohol at a friend's house. Her curiosity makes her want to learn more about the topic, but when her friend's dad gets into trouble because of it, she makes a vow. There are also facts in the story to help understand the issues relating to Alcohol.

Things Every Kid Should Know
Smoking!

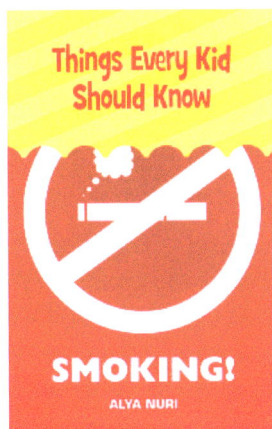

'Things Every Kid Should Know - Smoking!' will walk you through what Smoking is; why it is bad for you, and how to avoid picking up this bad habit. There is a story of two young friends who go through life, and what happens along their lives as they each make different choices. There are also facts in the story to help understand all the issues relating to Smoking.

Things Every Kid Should Know
Bullying!

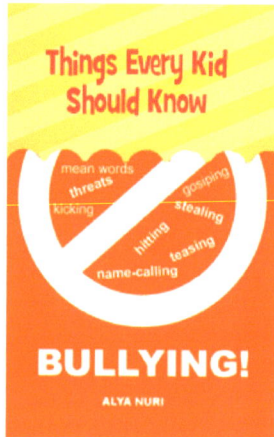

'Things Every Kid Should Know - Bullying!' will walk you through what Bullying is; why it is bad for you, and how to avoid picking up this bad habit. There is a story in this book to help kids learn what Bullying is all about. There are also facts in the story to help understand all the issues relating to Bullying.

www.ingramcontent.com/pod-product-compliance
Lightning Source LLC
Chambersburg PA
CBHW041307020426

42331CB00001B/3